Case Management 101:

Non-Clinical Tactics to Guide

Your Clients to Adequate Care

Developmental Disability Edition

Laketria Venzant

Case Management 101: Non-Clinical Tactics to Guide Your Client to Adequate Care by Laketria Venzant
© 2015 by Laketria Venzant. All rights reserved.

Published by: Tranquil Artistry LLC.
Interior Design by: Laketria Venzant
Cover Design by: Tra'Von Cooper
Editing by: Robert Carter Jr.
Creative Consultant: Robert Carter Jr.

Mailing, Laketria, 2016 – Case Management 101: Non-Clinical Tactics to Guide Your Client to Adequate Care

tranquilartistry@gmail.com

LCCN: 2016901747

ISBN: 978-0692540008
10 9 8 7 6 5 4 3 2 1
First Edition

CONTENTS

PREFACE

Congratulations! You've just received a call back stating you've been hired at a case management agency that serves clients with developmental disabilities. You're getting ready to embark on a journey that will allow you to advocate for individuals within your community. You're excited and cannot wait to start your new job. Only one problem; you've never worked in case management a day in your life and the job starts any day now. So, whether you've just graduated with your bachelor's degree, it's your first time foray into case management, or just returning to the workforce; you want to be prepared for the job. This book is just what you need. Of course, being a case manager can vary from agency to agency, but this book's sole purpose is to prepare you for what could possibly be your experience as a new case manager. I hope you find this content useful as well as a great reference for your new journey. Good Luck!

Chapter 1

What Do You Bring to the Table?

Before working with any population your employer may consider your personal attributes when working with clients in this field; because after all it's their reputation on the line and the last thing an agency needs is unwanted attention. When speaking of personal attributes several subjects come to mind. These can include the following: your can do attitude, patience in difficult situations, optimism, and advocate spirit. Take the time to see if these particular points are your strong suits and if they're not; try to find ways to address how you can make improvements in the future.

Can Do Attitude

The title speaks for its' self. When working within the area of case management you can possibly be left alone to figure out how to maintain a caseload early on. Meaning your ability to work independently is key and can potentially be your ticket to success. Important questions you may want to consider can include the following: Can you work well with others when conducting a meeting? Can you take the reins and show leadership and initiative when dealing with multiple entities? Can you see yourself being calm in a chaotic environment? Having a can do attitude can take you to the next level in the future, so take the attitude you approach your job with very seriously.

Patience

In **case management** this should be your first internal attribute because without it you can make things extremely difficult for yourself as well as your client. Understanding that a lot of things are out of your control should be your initial attitude in case management. For example, you have a client that is considered combative and has physically assaulted his **direct service worker**. Due to your client's behavior the **provider** wants to drop your client. This is his third provider agency in two years and he's built a reputation as being noncompliant. You have been put in a difficult position that requires a lot of your time. Not to mention you have thirty other clients that have necessary paperwork and issues of their own. Being patient and great with time management can create a more tranquil environment. Take advantage of downtime to work through your caseload.

*Great Tip: Talk to other case managers as to what tactics to use that will effectively keep you afloat with your caseload. It's common to feel impatient when things get out of control.

Glass Half Empty vs. Half Full (Optimism)

You as the case manager have to be optimistic and avoid being pessimistic as much as possible. You're working with clients on a daily basis that have barriers and challenges that prevent them from living their lives to full capacity. This could mean that your client may require assistance with daily living activities, independence, administering of medications, seeking employment, or being able to effectively interact with others within the community. Your job is not to say your client will never become capable of completing these goals, but what can you as well as the client's team put into place to in order for the client to better reach those goals. Even the smallest step towards independence can be monumental.

Possessing an Advocate Spirit

This is the most important personal attribute to have. When you have an advocate spirit you can determine whether or not your drive and passion for those that are unable to advocate for themselves is efficient and genuine. An advocate can be anyone; from a loved one who stands up for civil rights to the teenager that speaks publicly about bullying within the school system. Being an advocate can be rewarding to those that understand that change will not happen overnight, but every step is one step closer to their goal. Remember your goal is not to satisfy the provider, **caregiver**, and especially not your own personal gain or image, but it's the client's goal you are advocating for. There's no difference if the goals are big or small; you're there to speak and work for your client. Now that we have discussed your internal attributes; let's discuss educational and work background. You will be amazed by what is important and what I used to help me excel, and stay organized as a case manager.

Educational Background

When working with clients in this particular population, expect to see a lot of medical terms. This does not mean you are required to be a nurse in order to be an effective case manager. This just means that you should become more familiar with frequently used medical terms. Terms can include: prn, p.m., bi, prescribing information, side effects, mental/physical disorders, etc. Your client can possibly be a patient of a psychologist or psychiatrist and having a behavior plan is a part of your client's record. The more you familiarize yourself with this information the more at ease you will become with future clients.

On an average most, if not all case management agencies require their staff to have a bachelor's degree from an accredited university or college. The major concentrations that catch the employer eyes are: Psychology, Social Work, Sociology, Health & Human Services, and Criminal Justice. In the case you have a degree in another field you may still have a chance for the position. There is nothing wrong with trying. Your personal attributes and abilities could possibly be enough. When having a bachelor's degree in one of the afore mentioned majors, you my friend may have an advantage. You've been previously prepped and prepared to advocate and work with individuals that may have developmental disabilities. That brings me into the next subject, your work history.

Let's say you have a bachelor's degree in psychology and your work history includes working hands on with clients that have mental and/or physical disabilities; the employer may initially feel that they've hit the jackpot. For an employee to have work experience with an agency's population can be a great advantage to you as well as your employer. You possess a different advantage that other staff may have never experienced. You can honestly understand both sides of the spectrum in this field. You can understand the person that works as the direct staff worker (dsw) and can effectively see what their job entails as well as the specifications of boundaries as a direct staff worker. Now you have the opportunity to see the documentation side of providing the client with adequate care. Having that worker bee mentality and empathy gives you a fighting chance to look at the situation at a higher level. You are already ahead of the game with hands on work history. One thing to remember is to never compare your previous clients to your new clients. Every situation is different; make sure you treat them as such.

Now on to my secret that will help you further your success as a case manager. You remember in college there was a class that was dedicated to Microsoft Excel. Remember how you hated all the extra formulas and magical activity; where you would press a bottom and information would move and new dates would appear out of thin air. Well, that genie like activity can separate the kids from the adults in the case management world. You have to become accustomed to deadlines for several things simultaneously, while being a case manager. For example: **Comprehensive Plan of Care (CPOP)**, **transitioning** (aging out), **revisions, environmental modifications**, etc. The list goes on as well as your employer's expectations to keep everything up to date. Excel can be your savior as well as your own personal log of what you've completed and what is considered a priority. If you're reading this book before graduating; pay attention to the magical activity, it will soon pay off. Trust me.

Chapter 2

Understanding Your Population

This chapter will be a more in depth understanding of the population you will be providing a service to. When you're working with clients who have developmental disabilities you should first understand that this is a person who needs assistance. The client has the same rights as you and I. Understand that the person has a disability, but it should not limit them from receiving adequate care and/or resources. Familiarize yourself with individuals who have disabilities. You can accomplish this by volunteering for community entities that assist clients with disabilities or you can converse with others that have worked hands on with clients. Remember when receiving information from others use your best judgment because that person may only recall negative experiences that can contribute to your sense of anxiety. This can hinder you from providing the best possible care to your clients. So, make sure you learn as much as possible from as many resources as you can.

Familiarize yourself with their diagnosis. Again, this is a non-clinical approach to being a case manager, but due to the population, it's a common factor that you will have to become accustomed to seeing your client's diagnosis. First, try not to get overwhelmed by the diagnosis. When a client has been added to your caseload and you're working on their paperwork, it's very important to know all of the client's diagnosis. For instance, you have a client diagnosed with bipolar disorder and you have completed their paperwork to be reviewed and critiqued before starting services. You receive follow up questions from the reviewer asking if there were any other diagnosis. This is where you go back and ask the client and/or caregiver for additional information. While talking to the caregiver you've been informed that although your client has been diagnosed with bipolar disorder; the client has also been diagnosed with diabetes and hypertension. This would ultimately change your previous information. Instead of the client's objective/goal reflecting assistance and care for their bipolar disorder; now you would want to put into place nutritional guidelines suggested by their physician and possibly a quarterly visit to a podiatrist for preventative measures. Knowing all of your client's diagnosis is very important in providing a more detailed background of your client's health.

Understanding the Client's View of Independence

You have a male client that is 25 years old and wants to live alone. He is non-ambulatory and need twenty-four hour services. He has lived with his parents all his life and wants to experience independence. Your client is mentally capable of making his own decisions, but the parents are afraid of the unknown. Do you take the parents' side and try to convince your client that he should stay or do you go along with your client's request?

This is a great example of a client wanting their independence. In this field you will find a lot of parents and/or caregivers that devote their lives to their loved one's health and safety needs. When you become a skilled case manager, you can see the nonverbal cues of the parent wanting to protect their family member forever; but many neglect the thought that they themselves will not live forever. In most cases the family forgets to make preparations for their own death when caring for a disabled family member and some clients are left without any guidance as to what should be done in this situation. In the above example, you may want to side with the parent, but your goal is to make sure the health and safety of the client is first priority. If everything with health and safety is covered, you must present all options to the client and family members. Options could include the following:

Independent Living: where the client lives alone in their own house, apartment, or manufactured home.

Shared Supports: where the client lives with another client and share direct staff worker hours in order to provide adequate care for both clients.

Day Habilitation/Employment: where the client becomes involved in community activities with other clients for a set period of time during the day. This allotted time allows the client to interact with others within the community.

These are options to assist in providing the client with independence. This can ultimately help the client as well as address the subject of independence with the caregiver in a gradual way.

Understanding the Caregiver of a Developmentally Disabled Client

We touched on this subject in the previous sub-section, but this topic deserves more detail. In case management for this population the client may not be the issue. Your client loves when you make your home visits, enjoys keeping you aware of their milestones and achievements, and can be very cooperative to changes within the agency's policies and procedures. Remember the caregiver is also an essential part of the equation. Caregivers can be illustrated in different ways. One way to illustrate a caregiver is someone being the client's nature support. This could include the clients' mother, father, aunt, uncle, sister, or someone that has legal rights to discuss the client's health and/or finances. Natural supports can be easy, but at times they can be extremely difficult. So let's talk about both situations. First, you have the easy, natural supports. This caregiver responds to the client's needs in order to assist in providing adequate care. This could include taking on the remaining hours of care in order to provide the client with twenty-four-hour care. This caregiver understands that not in all cases will the client receive twenty-four-hour care through a funded program and they decide to pitch in and pick up the slack. This could also mean their awareness of the client's health issues and working as a team to come up with effective solutions to the problem. These are natural supports that want to help the process as much as possible.

Then there is the more challenging natural support. These could include natural supports that have no idea about the client's health issues. They criticize everything you, your agency, and/or provider do. They harass the direct worker staff constantly, but have no desire to work with the client themselves. These are just a few examples of what you may encounter. It's your job to keep the peace as much as possible when faced with challenging natural support. Your ultimate goal is to advocate for the client. You may not be the natural support, but you are a part of the team. When dealing with challenging natural support try to remember your main focus is your client.

Tip: Always document difficult situations. Remember in case management, if it is not recorded it did not happen.

There's one more natural support category to mention and it's the natural support from the beginning of the sub-section. This natural support has devoted their life to provide care for their loved one.

They are your client's first and greatest advocate. They will call you with changes to their medications, updated information, find resources with you, and want to protect the client from any harm. These are what I consider great advocates to have at your client's side. You as the case manager feel a sort of relief when talking to them because you know you're working as a team. Their only pitfalls are letting go and lack of preparation. They can sometimes feel as though they're the only one that can provide care to the client. In most cases, they're also hindering themselves from seeking options in the case that they themselves become ill or even die. You may feel the need to discuss this right away with the caregiver, but first build a rapport with them and then discuss all their options. You will be surprised as to how many parents well within elder adulthood still care for their adult children. Discussing a will or power of attorney should be a topic to help put their minds at ease, because trust me, although they never talk about it to you without prompting; they have at least thought about it themselves.

Chapter 3

Picking Up Where They Left Off

Their Desk.... Now Your Mess

You walk into the office on your first day and the supervisor points you to your desk. On the inside you want to scream because it looks as though the desk has been hit by a small tornado of unfiled paperwork, multiple copies of overly printed out forms, and sticky fingers from your new co-workers that have taken the good stapler and oversized calendar from your desk. All that is left is a pile of paperwork in every desk drawer and a telephone. You've been wondering to yourself how did I get in this situation and how can I keep my sanity. The following sub-sections will help you get started.

Paperwork

You and paperwork have to become best friends in case management. Like I stated before if it is not documented it did not happen. A lot of paperwork has now become electronic. This is to cut back on paper usage and everyone's arch nemesis, the filing system. In the case you're still required to manually do paperwork, it's best to start on the right track. So you're at your new desk and you're wondering where to start. You should start by organizing the papers that need to be filed. Just because the previous case manager neglected to file them; does not mean this process should be neglected on your part. You never know when an auditor may appear at the agency. The last thing you need is for there to be a gap in services and you have to fumble though a stack of papers for one piece of documentation. Create a filing system early on and stick to it as much as possible. Now you have all of your papers filed for each client; then there are the forms that have been printed 10-20 times. Take a manila folder and label them with the form's name and number. Trust me if it was printed 10-20 times then it must be a frequently used document. Now your desk is starting to clear and because you've filed away your clients' documents; you've become familiar with their names. Also, because you categorized your forms you're now familiar with those papers as well. You have now successfully created a beginning system for your caseload.

Creating Your System

From what you have completed previously; you're on the right track. Now you have been given your list of clients and you want to create a system for them as well. You may have to create not one, but several systems depending on your clientele. For example, you have a caseload of 35 clients. You can create an excel spreadsheet with different titles; which may include the following: CPOC end dates, residential location, birthday, quarterly visit date, and/or prioritized environmental modifications. Creating your personalized system helps to keep you on track; not just for yourself but also your clients. This could also help in the case you decide to no longer work for the agency. Passing this system along to others can help the new case manager pick up where you left off.

Deadlines: The Ghost of Case Manager's Past

You're having a great week. Your desk is organized and you've familiarized yourself with the documentation. You feel confident and ahead of the game. Then your supervisor comes in and wants to speak with you privately. She states that your caseload was left with several deadlines and the necessary paperwork has yet to be completed. She will help you with the clients that are considered a priority, but the remaining four you will be primarily left alone. You're now being thrown into the fire and now it's time to get to work. You've seen already what the previous case manager did not complete and you're wondering to yourself; what did they do for the last two weeks of employment? Well, that question is no longer important and it is now your job to pick up the slack and bring the caseload back up to par. The first thing is to remember your system. Put clients in order as to whose documentation is getting close to expiring. These clients are now your #1 priority. When working with your supervisor, never shadow empty handed. Your supervisor is used to the jargon and will expect for you to pick up on it quickly. So if you're informed to have the family complete form IFS-86; remember that form because it may become frequently used. Also, know and understand you're only one person and you can only do so many things at one time. Try to realize that the supervisor may want to provide you more one on one time, but cannot due to another obligation of his/her position. Use your co-workers for assistance. Try to socialize and get as much information (policy friendly) as possible. This will help fill in the gap from not having your supervisor for assistance. The previous case manager's work may linger, but it's your caseload now, so treat it as such.

Staying Within Policy & Procedure with the Client

You're still new at the agency as well as with your clients. You've become familiar with a lot of things in a short period of time. You're also becoming familiar with the way the previous case manager interacted with the clients. The previous case manager was obviously not organized and lacked a sufficient system. Your clients have become accustomed to seeing their case manager every 6 months instead of every 3 months, as stated in the policy and procedure book. During a visit to your client; they go on to state that the previous case manager had an understanding about the frequency of annual visits. By the looks of their home the client is in need of several resources and that if the case manager made adequate visits to the home would have been able to present assistance to the client. The client is adamant about keeping the same schedule and has stated that they have been in the "system" for so long that there is no need for any changes. Your policy and procedure clearly states you must make a quarterly visit to the client also including the provider in order to monitor services. So, what do you do?

Remember this is your caseload and that the previous case manager was obviously not following the mandated rules of the agency. You should feel empowered to inform the client that although the previous case manager may have handled the situation incorrectly; you will not put the client's health and safety at risk. Let the client know that you want to build a rapport with them and that meeting and talking about their concerns is a priority. Inform them that the agency has policies and procedures in place that must be followed under state and/or federal guidelines. You can safely assume that the client may not have been aware of these rules or that the previous case manager made breaking the rules seem ok. Nevertheless, you must break that cycle and represent yourself as well as the agency with the utmost integrity and respect.

Chapter 4

Expecting the Unexpected: Unrealistic Goals and Your Attempt to Reach Them

Your Caseload/Client

You're overwhelmed with your caseload. You have 35 clients and they all need your attention. You've been juggling quarterly meetings, annual paperwork, environmental modifications, provider agency issues, and to add on to the pile you have a complaint from one of your clients. You're in shock as to who the client is and cannot believe you're being called into the office by your supervisor. You feel a sense of anger and betrayal all at the same time. You're wondering what the complaint could possibly be about. Your supervisor goes on to state that the client feels you're not getting his staff more hours and that those additional hours are needed. Your anger turns for the worst as you begin to plead your case to your supervisor. The truth is that the client's staff is a friend of the family and they would like to work more hours, although your client does not need any additional hours. This would only serve your client's staff as an easy monetary gain. Your client has no current health or safety issues in order to report an addendum to your documentation. You have other clients that require your attention and this is the last thing you need. This is one example of expecting the unexpected. When you think everything is fine and you're hit with unsettling information that can throw you off task. Remember prioritization is key. Start with getting a meeting together with all parties and try to provide as many options as possible. If the staff needs additional hours, then the provider should be made aware so that other arrangements can be made and not at the expense of your client.

Agency

You are already seeing firsthand how things can change at any time while working with clients. Understand that these situations are out of your control and you must handle them the best way possible. Agencies vary in many different ways and the variation can create positive as well as negative changes within the agency. One critical way is financially, if an agency has financial issues, this could change something as small as how many copies you make all the way to something as large as layoffs. Understand that in some cases, it's out of your employers control as to how much they would like to keep things the same, it can sometimes be impossible. Try to consider their standpoint and take into consideration that everything may not be as clean cut underneath the surface.

Government/Federal

You can somewhat have control over your caseload and the possible changes. Even when it comes to the agency you can choose to stay or terminate your employment. But let's say your state has cut a Medicaid funded entity and will no longer be considered a resource after the next 30 days. You have clients that use those resources and the troubling information has added to an already overwhelming situation. Try to remember that the rules can change at any time in case management. Never get too comfortable with government policies and procedures; you must always be acceptable to change.

Chapter 5

Networking: Community Supports & Resources

Freedom of Choice

As a case manager, you will gradually pick up on community resources. This is a way to better serve your clients. Get used to receiving business cards for future references. Hopefully the agency you work for will allow you to use business cards as well. This could also help you put your name out into the community as an advocate for services. There were plenty of times where I received phone calls from someone that knew a client that I previously helped and they were gracious enough to pass my name along. Networking with clients can be a little tricky. In the Medicaid arena, there's something called a **Freedom of Choice**. This is basically a list of categorized resources that are designated for Medicaid recipients. The list can entail **personal care attendant** providers, environmental modification contractors, **respite care entities**, and the list go on. It is ingrained into case managers early on that you are not to persuade a client and/or caregiver to use a particular company. This act is very much frowned upon, especially from agencies that are not given a chance to provide services. Also, you as the case manager open the opportunity to receive backlash from the client/caregiver if the agency you pick was insufficient. No matter if you had a difficult time with the resource entity; you should leave the choice up to your client. In the case the client is adamant about you picking the resource; stay firm with your words and leave the decision up to the client.

Surrounding Resources

Just like your client, you as the case manager need to know all resources within the area. Your clients have a variety of barriers, so your job is to network as much as possible to address those barriers. Get familiar with community supports in your area. This could range from monthly activities for your clients or neighborhood entities that do annual giveaways to clients that fit the resources' criteria. Always express yourself as an advocate and retrieve as much information as possible. You will find in most cases that the information you receive cannot only help your client, but others that may be in need of the same resources.

Online Research

You will find that online resources are great. It is your way of casting a larger net for your clients' needs. Online you can find agencies that can help with purchasing corrective eyewear for low income families all the way to refurbished computers for client with developmental disabilities. Online resources are everywhere, but make sure you do your research in order to avoid scams. The last thing you would want is for the agency that you suggested; to use your client's information in any unauthorized way. Online resources can also be great because it doesn't require you to leave your desk. You can do all of the searching right from your computer; which is always a plus.

Informing the Client of Activities

In this field of case management, you will find a lot of your clients may lack chances for community activities. This could be due to a number of things, but it is up to you to make an effort to inform your client of any activities within their community. Whether there's a local game event or even a party where your client can meet and socialize with others; make a call to your client and/or caregiver to inform them in advance of the activity and make a point to follow up. You will realize that in some cases their support system may not be aware of any community activities. With this you can create a rapport with the client to increase their awareness for future community events.

Networking According to the Clients and/or Caregivers Needs

You have a client that is currently learning sign language at their school. This is one of the strengths that you have noted in your documentation. As you're updating information during a quarterly meeting; the client's mother states she wants to learn sign language as well as but she has no idea where to start. She comes to you for help. What do you do? This is a great example where you use your better judgement. The mother is very interested in effectively communicating with her child. This is very important for the client to be able to express their needs within their household. Make a point to look for sign language classes as well as pertinent information to relay over to the mother. In the case it's something she cannot afford try to find Medicaid entities that can assist with the cost for the class. Make sure that the mother fits the criteria of the resource. This is your way of helping your client as well as the family. You will find in many cases it will be the family that will request assistance on behalf of the client. Use your better judgement before stating that the client qualifies for a particular service. In the case you're unsure, ask your supervisor for assistance. Remember, you have other clients on your caseload and you want to avoid wasting time as much as possible.

*Great Tip: An example of an exception would be if the family is constantly lifting the client independently and they themselves have health issues of their own. Understand they are your client's natural support and this will help the family as well as the client. Again, use your better judgment.

Chapter 6

Staying Focused: Office Etiquette

Socializing in the Office

Understand that although you are an advocate, this is still a job. Keep in mind that everyone at the agency may not have the same drive and ambition as you. They are only there to receive a paycheck. It is only 4:25p.m. and they are already packed and ready to go home. To be perfectly honest, some co-workers are already headed to their vehicles. Know that socializing at the office is great in some cases, but it can be a hindrance in others. For instance, you just started your day and you hear your co-worker talking about they have no plans of doing any working for the day and that even though it's 8:15am; they're already tired. Try your best to keep your socializing to a minimum. As time goes on you will begin to notice the one's that hover around other office doors, never stay at their desk, and always in the middle of office gossip. These are the co-workers that never seem to understand why they have yet to receive their annual raise. When you start your job just sit back and analyze the workplace dynamic. You will soon figure out the office pet, trouble maker, slacker, and so on. Now I'm not saying become the nonverbal weirdo in the corner office, but just try to be aware of your surroundings.

Notice the Frequently Called Co-Worker

You will be in the middle of working at your desk and realize that one of your co-workers has been called into the supervisor's office several times. You see the stress on their faces every time they pass your desk. In some cases, when in case management you wonder how do they still have a job? You've heard that their deadlines are never met, clients constantly complain, and they lack organization within their caseload. They come in with a smile on their face and by the end of the day they internally cringe at the sound of their supervisor calling their name. This is the person you never want to be. In most cases, these are employees that have fallen behind and cannot seem to catch up. They refuse to work extra hours just because they are only get paid for eight. In their eyes, that's the maximum they're willing to work. They constantly complain and talk to others about how they wish they could quit but need the money. You will notice in some cases their supervisor and other employees will attempt to help them, but to them, it's an impossible uphill battle and it's just too much for them to take on. This employee can be seen in any field, but in case management this lack of consistency can result to clients having a gap in services and unnecessary paperwork being completed. Try to stay on task and avoid being the frequently called co-worker.

Lunch Break Turns to Client Bashing

You've built a rapport with your co-workers and you've agreed to join them at a local Italian restaurant. The restaurant is known for having a great lunch special with a spectacular lasagna dish. You and your co-workers take a seat in the packed restaurant and then out of nowhere one of your co-workers begin to talk about the home visit they have in the upcoming week. Your co-worker states the client's name, then go on to talk about how filthy the house is and that she hates going there. She goes on to state that she's going to try to get the family to have a quick meeting on the porch. Upon returning to the office you all are called into the director's office and the verbal reprimands begin. As you all are dismissed back to work the employee that discussed the client's information is informed that the client's aunt was at the table next to yours and wants the employee to receive disciplinary action for her hurtful words and has requested that the client received another case manager immediately. Do you think the aunt has any right to be angry? Yes, your co-worker was very negligent with the client's information. This is an example of how something as simple as a lunch break can take a turn for the worst. The client as well as the caregiver will lose their ability to trust the employee and possibly the agency. When you're in public, whether it's with co-workers or not you never know who's listening. You must always think of your client's well-being and protect their information. Never leave their information unattended when out in the community. Talking to those that are not privileged to your client's information can be a HIPPA violation. Take time to consider your surroundings, even within the office when an office guest or potential client may be around.

Chapter 7

Mid Book Recap

These are just a few tips that were mentioned earlier in the book. Hopefully these particular tips will be of some assistance while working in case management.

- Know what your greatest attributes are for the interview.

- You have a great advantage in this field of case management if you have a bachelor's degree in the following: psychology, social work, sociology, or criminal justice.

- Try out volunteering for organizations that assist individuals who have developmental disabilities. Also, it would be great to have hands on experience with the population.

- Understand that picking up where the previous case manager left off is not the time to reflect on what has yet to be completed, but how can you bring the caseload up to speed.

- Get organized as possible. Use an excel spreadsheet to your advantage to help recognize deadlines.

- Prioritize your caseload.

- Stay calm and familiarize yourself with your client and your new desk.

- Never be afraid to ask for assistance from your supervisor and/or co-workers.

- Remember, you're only one person and you can only do so much.

- Get familiar with policy and procedure for the agency.

- Expect changes with the caseload, agency, and federal entities. Always expect the unexpected.

- Use all available resources for assisting your clients. For online resources do your research about the organization for scams.

- Try to keep you socializing to a minimum in the office. Remember your job is to advocate for the client not waste time socializing with co-workers on the clock.

- Always keep in mind of your surroundings when discussing clients. You never know who's listening.

- Documentation, documentation, documentation. This goes for the client, natural support, provider, and etc. Remember if it is not documented it did not happen.

***Also keep personal documentation of any meetings with your supervisor. Communication through e-mails should be saved in order to keep a paper trail.

Chapter 8

Initial Meeting Process: Basic Tips

Beginning, Middle, and End

I'm sure you're wondering why this is one of the later chapter's in the book. This chapter is connected to the next two chapters that will get you better prepared for meeting with your client. The book starts with meeting clients with your supervisor as well as reaching the point of helping them with their goals and resources. This chapter is just to give you a more in-depth insight as to what that beginning meeting should include.

Before you leave the office to meet your client. Your first task is preparation. In preparing to meet with the client make sure you make a courtesy call explaining to the client that you will be making a home visit. During this phone call let the client know what the visit is for and the approximate time you will need to complete the meeting effectively. Try to get all documentation prepared the day before your meeting. Getting your documentation together can assist in eliminating the chances of unnecessary home visits due to your negligence of forgetting important documentation. Thus, costing the agency more money for mileage. Another aspect of preparation is time management. Your client will be greatly pleased if you were to be time. The last thing you need is for your client to address your tardiness before inviting you into their home. Next, when you arrive at your client's home show the client that you're happy to meet them. This gives the client a chance to feel at ease with a stranger entering their home. If they're a veteran client; they are more than likely use to case managers entering and accessing their home. Just remember that giving a smile and a handshake can make the initial process easier. Also, address the client as mister or miss; unless they request otherwise. Being polite does go a long way. Next, explain again to the client why you're there and the approximate length of time you will need in order to complete important paperwork. During the meeting start with reviewing where the last case manager left off. This will work as a refresher to the client as well as other team members as to what was stated at the last meeting. If the client and/or team have new information or concerns; make a note of what they're saying. If this is your first time conducting a meeting alone and the client request something you're unsure about; take a note and state that you will check on it when you get back to the office. This way you're addressing their concerns and not dismissing them. Stay away from setting things in stone that you're not sure about. This can create trust issues with your client. Next tip, remember why you're there. You be surprised as to how fast people within the meeting can quickly get off task. If it's an initial intake meeting tell the client about all the services, you can provide as well as what you cannot provide. Let them know in advance what's considered mandatory for you as well as the agency. This will help the client understand that these things are necessary in order to receive and continue services. This could also include mandatory home visits, phone calls, documentation, etc. Getting your client and/or caregiver mentally prepared for semi-annual or annual visits can decrease their chances of feeling overwhelmed by what they may have previously felt was unnecessary and unexpected rules/visits. After you have held the meeting, always do a recap of any concerns or needs the client may have mentioned. Reassure them of an approximate date you will return with answers to their concerns. This will help keep all parties on track. End your meeting by scheduling for the next meeting with all parties. Say your friendly goodbyes and leave their home confident that you can assist the client with reaching their goals. More importantly, they should feel as if you can and will advocate for them.

Now you're back at your desk and you're wondering where to start. The first thing you have to do is document your visit. Every agency is different as to how much detail you have to put into your notes. The best advice to give to a new employee is to put as much detail as possible and try to continue doing so throughout your time as a case manager. Keep in mind that you will become very busy and may not want to document everything but it cannot be said enough; if it is not documented it did not happen.

Documentation Example:

Case manager went out to the home for a quarterly meeting. Attendees for the meeting were: John (client), Martha (mother), Stan (provider facilitator), Tiffany (direct service worker), and Maggie (aunt). The meeting included updates from the client's mother stating that his medications have changed. Metformin is now 500mg and Lisinopril is now 40mg. We discussed his diabetes and nutritional status. It was agreed that his eating habits were out of control. His mother and dsw will work with him to start cooking healthier meals and walk 2-3 times per week. Case manager informed the team that an addendum will be made to his comprehensive plan of care reflecting John's goal to increase instances of eating healthier and exercising. All parties agreed to meet again in 3 months on August 5th at 2:30pm. No other concerns nor complains were stated.

Sounds extensive, right. Well let's say for instance you forgot to mention his change in medications and went on without making changes to John's plan. It would look as though everything's fine and no changes were reported about his health for three months. At that point the next time you will meet with them again will be six months later. A lot of changes can happen with your client within six months let alone one month. With your notes you are able to keep track of John's health and safety. As well as to what John's staff is doing and if she's assisting him with his daily living activities. So let's say for instance you return three months later only to find out that the client has refused to exercise and has yet to change his eating habits, you as the case manager have no control over what the client should do. It's the client's right to refuse to work toward his or her goals. You as the case manager should document the information and make suggestions to the client and team members to try other tactics in order to assist the client. This may include 1-2 walks per week instead of 2-3. Any progress is better than no progress.

Chapter 9

Safety & Boundaries with Your Clients

Case Manager: The Worker and Friend?

To your clients you are the person that helped them when no one else could. They call you about their needs and 9 times out of 10 you deliver. You're never rude and you always have a welcoming attitude. You're almost like family and to some of your clients; and in some cases you may very well be the only visitor during the annual holiday season. You've been there to wish them a happy New Year, Happy Easter, and talk about the heat during the summer. You yourself have come accustomed to your clients and feel as though their lives are a part of your life as well. This is the relationship you want with all of your clients, right?

Yes, and no, in some cases you as a case manager can become too close to your client. This can possibly create boundary issues. You can soon go from a case manager that talks to your client once a month in order to get important information about their health and safety to talking for an hour about their favorite television show, complaining about their staff's cooking, or how their neighbor is too loud. So how can you prevent this boundary issue?

First, provide friendly reminders to your client as to what specific times are dedicated to them. This will let the client know you have their concerns in mind, but you have other clients as well. Make a point to talk to their provider facilitator to have them address things that are under the umbrella of their expertise (ex: dsw cooking). Try to stay away from invites after hours. If it's an event where other case managers will be there (ex: tournament events); these are fine, but every Sunday dinner is overstepping your boundaries as a professional. Always remember you're a case manager that helps the client to increase their quality of life and to assist them to live as independently as possible. You're not there to become their best friend.

The Obsessive Client

Every so often a case manager tells a story about a client that was obsessed with them. In most cases they did their job well and never overstepped their boundaries. They know their limits and abide by their agencies' policy and procedure. But their client had a tendency of calling excessively. The client would constantly talk about the case manager's appearance and would try to flirt with them during every home visit. What would you do?

You should first let your client know that the behavior is inappropriate for the client and case manager relationship. Inform your supervisor of the clients' advances. **Document any occurrences** of their behaviors and if it gets to the point where you feel uncomfortable, ask that the client be removed from your caseload. Remember, you may have difficult clients, but when you feel your safety is at risk always follow your first mind.

Meeting Tips

Below are tips to use when conducting a meeting. Always remember to logically think about your safety and surroundings.

- **Avoid having lengthy meetings after office hours. Meaning, if it's 5:30pm and it takes you 30-45 minutes to get to the client's resident and the meeting may take longer than an hour; you should try to make those meetings in the morning or after your lunch break.**

- **Consider the location when scheduling your meeting.**

- **If the neighborhood is unsafe, try to visit during daylight hours.**

- **Try to avoid meeting on weekends. This is due to if any issues that may arise; you can call the office for assistance.**

- **Avoid arguing with the client and/or family member. If you're having issues that can escalate, try to set a time where your supervisor or another co-worker can accompany you. Not all meetings will require other team members.**

- **If your client has a history of being combative make sure you pay close attention to nonverbal cues (ex: rapid breathing, blank stare, self-infliction, sudden pica outburst, or rapid movements).**

- Never feel afraid to contact the police and or proper authorities when you've witnessed abuse or neglect.

- Keep a safe distance if you sense danger, stay in visual sight of an exit, and try to keep a cell phone with you at all times.

Chapter 10

Pulling it All Together: Case Examples

You've read the previous information and now you should have a sense of understanding about the basics. As previously stated in every agency that provide case management; services may vary. They can vary from the agency, state, and federal level. Every state has their own specified name for waiver services. In the state of Louisiana there are several waiver services for individuals with developmental disabilities. Waiver services could include **Children's Choice**, **New Opportunity Waiver**, **Residential Opportunity Waiver**, and **Supports Waiver**. Each has its own specified rules and guidelines. For research purposes, you should review your state's support and service options for people with disabilities. As a quick review, here are minor details of the above waiver services. This will give you as the case manager a better understanding as to what steps are taken in order to effectively address the case scenarios within this chapter.

Clients who receive assistance are clients that are medically diagnosed as having a disability. This could include clients that are born with a disability, who have become ill, or have been involved in an accident. Although there may be families in need of assistance; in some cases, families may have to be put on a waiting list for services. In some cases, it could take years before funds are available and new clients can receive assistance.

Waiver Service Background

Children Choice:

- Birth to 18 years old
- $19,000+ annual allotment of funds
- Covers the cost of dsw staff hours, environmental modifications, and/or other family necessities (ex: durable medical supplies/equipment).
- At 18 years old they must age out of Children's Choice Waiver and transitioned to the New Opportunity Waiver
- Additional Options Apply

NOW Waiver:

- Generally, 18 years old to older adult, but children have been known to receive NOW services before the age of 18
- More dsw hours
- If approved the client could receive 24-hour service (must meet criteria)
- Environmental Modifications
- Supported Independent Living (SIL) which is where the provider assists with the clients' finances
- Employment Assistance
- Respite Care
- Additional Options Apply

Supports Waiver

- Day Habilitation
- Respite Care

- Employment Assistance
- These clients are more independent and dsw hours are not needed
- Additional Options Apply

Residential Opportunity Waiver

- **Respite Care**
- **Personal Emergency Response System PERS**
- **Shared Living**
- **Supported Employment**
- **Day Habilitation**
- **Additional Options Apply**

There are more services within Louisiana to assist disabled individuals. These are just a few to help you better understand the process for the following case scenarios. As stated before, every agency is different, but these are possible tactics to use in order to address case situation.

Read the case scenario independently or with your supervisor and discuss what you would do. These are just examples to help you critically think about how to address situations as they arise.

Case Scenario #1: Aging Out Client

Beverly has been a case manager at ABC Case Management for almost a year now. She has a caseload of 34 clients that vary in waiver programs. She has paperwork and deadlines to keep and she wants to stay ahead. Beverly is called into her supervisor's office and she's been given another client to add to her caseload. Jason Smith is a 17-year-old Caucasian male who's currently a Children's Choice recipient. He currently lives with his adopted parents in a rural area. He's diagnosed with Moderate Intellectual Disability, Obsessive/Compulsive Disorder, and Pica. A note to remember is that Jason is also nonverbal. You've had three visits with Jason and his family. You have observed that he's a polite young man and when you visit the home he's usually watching television or spending time in his room. The provider as well as the DCFS Department of Children and Family Services case worker wants to meet with all parties to discuss his future after turning 18 years old. Jason's birthday is in 9 months and everyone wants to discuss the options that are available. It was agreed that the team has 9 months to get Jason set up for transition. Here are his options: (1) Jason's adoptive parents can continue to let Jason live with them. (2) Shared Supports with another client. (3) Try to get Jason approved for 24-hour service and move him into his own home. (4) Move Jason to a residential facility that provides 24-hour service. * If Jason moves into a residential facility, he may lose his slot with his transition to NOW Waiver. We will go over every option in-depth, so that you as the employee can see all possibilities.

Option #1: Adopted Parents

You as well as the team have to address every option possible. The first option is to ask the adoptive parents if the client can continue to live with them. For this example, the parent stated that they were not interested in letting the client stay after turning 18 years old. Understand it's their right to not provide your client with a continuous living arrangement. So we will move on to the other options.

Option #2: Shared Supports

This would involve you as well as the team possibly doing extended work and research for resources. First, there's finances. You will have to address his need for receiving SSI, SNAP benefits, and possibly housing assistance (HUD Housing or Section 8). Next, is finding a client that Jason can share supports with. For instance, it's in the best interest of clients that they are somewhat compatible. This makes it easier, so that both clients are happy and continue with their goal of having the best quality of life. You wouldn't want to pair a client that's combative and disruptive with a quiet and mild mannered client. This would prevent the client from maintaining his happiness. So compatibility is very important.

Option #3: Individual 24 Hour Services

With this option you're addressing the same thing as option #2 except you're preparing the client to live alone. Whether it's in a house, apartment, or manufactured home. Keep in mind that with this option, it can be very costly. You as the case manager have to figure in many factors within his budget, and by budget I'm not referring to his personal funds, but what it will cost to provide his services annually through the waiver services. Everything has a price. So let's say in order for Jason to live alone with 24-hour service 7 days a week, **SIL**, day habilitation, and case management fees; it all comes out to approximately $110,000 annually. These are services that Jason needs annually in order to live a better quality of life. This is only for one individual so let's factor in the cost if it were two people under the same roof. The codes for the budget will change and it would be more cost effective for the state if shared support is used. Your goal is to maintain the client's health and safety, but also try to be as cost effective as possible.

Option #4: Declining NOW Waiver Services for Facility Residency

This option may require the client to give up his slot with the NOW Waiver. This is a very big decision because the waiting list for other clients wanting services can be long as well as lengthy when considering the amount of time, they have to wait to receive services. In some cases, it could be years. So if your client gave up his slot and for whatever reason things within the facility don't work out it's imperative that he immediately has those services restored, but how long will the wait be. At the facility, there's no need for SNAP benefits nor housing assistance. He will receive three meals a day and social interaction with other clients. But consider the fact that Jason has never lived in a facility and it will be a big adjustment for him. Every option has its great points and pitfalls. Understand that you have to look at the situation from all angles.

Case Scenario #2: Combative Client

You have a caseload of 34 and a new client has been added to your caseload. Tommy Doe is a 35-year-old male. He's a recipient of the NOW Waiver services. Tommy's diagnosis is Mild Intellectual Disability and bipolar disorder. He lives alone in a one-bedroom apartment in a great neighborhood. He's been a tenant there for over 2 years. The landlord is aware of his disabilities and he is welcomed with no issues nor concerns. Tommy was approved for 24-hour service due to his combative behaviors. Tommy has been in trouble with authorities for vandalism, trespassing on private property, indecent exposure, and assault. He's known to have a quick temper and he's currently taking medications daily to assist him with suppressing his anger. He likes to be left alone to watch his favorite television shows and hates going out to crowded social events. At the quarterly meetings for the past year there were no issues reported in his documentation. Everything seems to be in order. Two weeks after your last quarterly meeting, you receive a call from Tommy's panicking provider stating that Tommy has damaged the property in his apartment. She goes on to state that he was angry that the staff asked him to clean his room. She stated he began to get combative with the staff, which resulted in the staff going to the hospital and he's now receiving worker's compensation. They have sent in another male staff and Tommy's behavior seems to have gotten worse. Tommy's neighbors have complained to the landlord about Tommy's disruptive behavior and now he's on the verge of losing his apartment. His provider is at the end of her rope and thinks that Tommy is a liability. She asks for an immediate team meeting. Where do you start with this case?

Understand that you may have clients like Tommy or even more difficult. Being able to critically think on your client's behalf is a must in case management. Here are some options you should try to consider.

Option #1: Address Any Changes

After having the client on your caseload for a while and after looking at the previous documentation; ask yourself as well as team members what has changed. Changes could range from non-consistency with medications, dsw staff, changes in routine, changes in neighbors, or maybe a doctor visit is needed. Sometimes a simple doctor visit with an adjustment to the medication can help.

Option #2: Investigation

Remember, you can take on many hats as a case manager, which could include being an investigator. Look at all details. Read the direct staff workers' notes. Notice any changes from shift to shift. See what the communication process is between staff. You will be surprised as to how many people work together and dislike each other. Even to the point of not doing their job, not relaying over shift information properly, or trying to create a widget between the client and other staff. This can result to the client feeling as though they should take sides, thus creating an unsafe environment. So let's say you find out that there are two issues going on his Tommy's household. (1) The client has not been taking his medication. (2) The staff is going to war over issues within the client's home. Morning and evening staff feel that the night shift staff is lazy and they have decided to work together to get him fired. Which is the reason the client has become combative with the night shift staff and he's refused to take his medication at night. Seems far-fetched, right. Well expect the unexpected, you may end up in the middle of several fires when dealing with your client's team and have to put them out. So what steps would you take to rectify the situation so your client can get his life back on track and avoid eviction? I will include a few options to consider.

Option #1: Medication Adherence

You as the case manager must explain to the provider and the team that health and safety is the utmost goal for the client. Ask if the client has an upcoming doctor's appointment and if not request that one be made immediately to address the gap in medication.

Option #2: Staff Clarification

Although this is the provider's area. You still have to address your concerns and what steps will be taken to change the situation. This could include changing the staff to another home or termination. Putting the client in this situation is unacceptable and should be addressed. Due to their issues and not discussing it properly with their supervisor could have been extremely dangerous for your client. Set the tone in a professional manner that this behavior will not be tolerated.

Understand that as a case manager, you will wear many hats. Try to look at each case from a different angle. Also, remember as stated before always document when and if situations like this escalate. Document as much as possible about the meeting and what you found during the review of their documentation. Remember, if it's not documented it didn't' happen.

I hope these two case scenarios helped you look at situations from a different standpoint. Although there were options and suggestions given; the rules and regulations always change. Make sure you refer back to your agency for more guidance.

Chapter 11

Handling Repetition: You Lose One to Gain Another

The last three chapters of this book will be dedicated to you, the reader. You have taken on a great responsibility as an advocate. You need as many tips as possible to stay on track with your job. Take time to get familiar with some of the tips in these chapters, they may come in handy.

The Big Elephant in the Room: Different Year, Same Life/Revolving Door

You've been a case manager at your job for going on three years. You've assisted countless clients in achieving their goals. Some have aged out and have been passed on to other case managers or even passed away due to natural causes. You have been an asset to society by helping others. You finally have your caseload under control. You have 40 clients and you are for once on top of your game. No issues that you cannot handle have been reported by your clients. You've built a rapport with them and their team members, so now all you do is your quarterly and annual visits in order to maintain services. Everything is great, actually too great. You've heard around the office that there will be changes, but no announcements have been made;

until today. Your supervisor calls you into her office to state that she's taking 10 clients from your caseload and replacing them with new ones. Thus, taking you from the familiar to the unfamiliar. Now you have to start over with a practically new case load. You start to feel the tension and your neck begins to tighten. The door was almost closed, but someone kicked it open and now it feels as though every client in the state has taken a number to be on your caseload. If you're a long time case manager, you're aware of the revolving door routine. So here are a few tips to assist you with the revolving door.

Tip #1: Take deep breaths and clear your mind during down time.

Tip #2: During down time get up from your desk. If it's a sunny day step outside feel the breeze and appreciate the simple things for a second.

Tip #3: Try tranquility music at your desk. Whether it's low volume rain, wind, or even soft jazz. It can help bring down the tone. You'll be surprised at how even with it playing in the background how it can help.

Tip #4: Seating. If it's in the budget for the agency, ask for a new chair. Seating can make a big difference. Nothing's wrong with asking, the worst they could say is no, right.

Tip #5 Take your vacations. Yes, you may have a pile of work when you get back, but a few days at a resort or somewhere with tropical drinks with little umbrellas can make a world of difference. Remember life will go on whether or not you're there. 2-3 days off isn't a full vacation, but it's a start.

Tip #6 Do not forget who you are. Yes, you're a case manager. Yes, you're an advocate. Yes, you want to let your work speak

for you, but you're still your own person. Remember, you have a life outside of work. Whether it's kids, loved ones, or hobbies, you're still you, so continue to be just that, you.

Avoiding Negatively

When you've been at an agency for years and you have the same clients, same co-workers, and same supervisors; it can become repetitive. This could contribute to you becoming negative. Have you ever encountered that co-worker that's been at the job so long that nothing the agency, their clients, the government, or even the world can do is right? Yes, you have, what may even be the case is that the person being mentioned may very well be you. Taking on a repetitive job can eat at you so subliminally that you won't be able to notice that you've become the negative energy in the room. So, what do you do about it and how to avoid instances of becoming a negative Nelson/Nancy?

Tip#1 Realize that your negativity can be draining to your environment. Being the negative one in the room can really change the dynamic of a situation.

Tip #2 Try to be more optimistic than pessimistic. Look at the situation from a more pleasant point of view.

Tip #3 Work on keeping your negative comments to a minimum. This will decrease instances of creating additional stress to an already stressful situation.

Tip #4 Smile and laugh more. Happiness can ease the soul.

Tip #5 (Repeat) Get up from the desk and go outside. Change your environment for a minute or two. Get some fresh air.

Tip #6 Realize that new employees have no need to hear how you've been at the agency for years and you basically feel sorry for them for accepting the position. This shows that you have created a negative space within yourself and that you feel the need to share any negative comments with anyone in sight. Making it seem as though you need someone to be as negative as you are. Being this way can make you closed minded and can potentially be harmful when working with clients. If this is you try to reevaluate your priorities and assess whether or not, you should stay at the job. Maybe it's your time to leave.

Take the time to review these tips. These are ways to help you during those difficult times when you may feel overwhelmed. The next two chapters will continue with tips for helping you become a better case manager.

Chapter 12

Avoiding Judgment: Kicking Your Biased Ways to the Curb

In a previous chapter the subject of understanding your population was addressed. It was important that attention be brought to that subject because every population must be handled differently. Yes, some aspects are blended from one population to the next, but they each have their own set of characteristics. In this chapter we will talk about you and how you interact with a population that has a multifaceted background for each client and how to work with those clients and still advocate for them.

Case Management: Is This the Job for You?

You have a new client that has been discharged from a facility for individuals with developmental disabilities. You've been given his paperwork and you realize that he's diagnosed with moderate Intellectual Disabilities and he's a pedophile. For the life of you, you can't understand how he's been discharged and being put back into the community. You're his new case manager and have to start on his plan of care right away. You're angry, upset, and disgusted by him and you've never seen his face. You go to your supervisor to get him immediately removed from your caseload. Your supervisor says no to your request and states that every case manager's caseload is full at the moment. What do you do?

First, this situation is very common. You will come in contact with clients that have lived or are living a lifestyle you do not personally agree with. You may have a pedophile, previous inmate, arsonist, or possible murderer. These clients have all different backgrounds and it's your job to provide a service to them. If you have a strong feeling that your client's background will prevent you from providing adequate services, then you should really consider if this is the job for you. Know that your personal beliefs are just that "your" personal beliefs. Being bias to your clients can be harmful to them as well as others within the community.

Case Scenario

Sam Smith is diagnosed with pedophilia and is a registered sex offender. You receive him as a new client and you're instantly upset because you have children. You meet with him and the team, but you make it known your dislike to the client's diagnosis. While walking outside with the provider agency's supervisor, the client over hears you talking negatively about him stating you're disgusted by the looks of him. During your following meetings you as well as the client continue to have anger stares at each other. In the meeting the client has stated that he's taking his medications, but neglects to state his urges to team members. You have created a space where honest has been put on the back burner. Thus creating an atmosphere where your client lacks a rapport that's needed in order for you to provide adequate services. Due to your negligence your client could potentially do something harmful to others as well as himself. Is this situation worth it just because of your bias ways? This is detrimental during the helping process. You have to step back and ask yourself is this the job for you? You have little or no control over the kind of clients you receive. So have a thick skin and try being diverse in your tactics of handling different situations. If you feel this job is too much for you, let your supervisor know about your concerns. Talk about how you feel. More than likely they will express to you the fact that this is a part of the job and that you have to deal with it. If that's the response you get, then go over the pros and cons and make your most educated decision. Remember, it's your decision to remain employed by the agency. You can find other ways to advocate if it's your decision to seek other employment.

Dealing with the Client's Past/Present Behavior

So, you decided to stay. Great! I know you still have a problem with your client's past. So let's go over a few tips to assist you with your dilemma.

Tip #1 Maintain your client/worker relationship. You still need to build a rapport with your client. Meaning you still have to use your same attending skills that you would use with any other client.

Tip #2 Go into the meeting being optimistic about your client achieving their goals.

Tip #3 Talk about any concerns you may have with your supervisor. Whether it's how uncomfortable you feel or if you feel out of control. Talk to your supervisor in order to help you get back on track.

Tip #4 Document... document... document. If you're in a situation where the client is making you feel uncomfortable document the occurrences.

Tip #5 If it's an unsafe situation always use your better judgment. Never endanger yourself and try to have a meeting with the team or when others are present. (DSW staff or caregiver)

If you've noticed that some of the tips are repetitive; it's presented that way for a reason. You as the reader need to recognize the importance of some of the content in this book and work on retaining that information for future references. Although, being a great case manager is key, being a safe one is better.

Chapter 13

You Are Making a Difference: Encouragement

You have been successfully prepped and prepared for employment at your new job. Take time to feel at ease that you are slightly more prepared than before. You can recognize your strengths, how to be a great case manager, how to pay attention to detail, and the list goes on. I want you as the reader to know that you are making a difference. You're the entity that connects your client to resources. You're the entity that makes sure other entities stay on track because they know you're watching. You expect others to do their due diligence for your clients just as much as you do. You're taking the word advocate and giving others a helping hand in recognizing their inner advocate without themselves being aware. You're changing lives and it's not for your betterment, but for that of the community. Know that there will be difficult situations, but you're the right person for the job. You're not there for the money and it's made clear with every phone call you make all the way down to your detailed documentation. You have perfected the ability to paint a picture of any situation that you describe on paper and you always have notes. You're not perfect, but you strive to be the best at your job. You help your co-workers in making their job as easy as possible by sharing your tactics and skills, not as competition but as an example of advocacy for all. You possess all of these abilities and you're just a new employee and all you brought to the table was your personal attributes, work history, and educational background. Put what you've read in this book to work and go on to advocate for change in your community one client at a time.

Glossary of Terms

caregiver – a person that is considered the client's family. Caregivers can be mother, father, sister, aunt, etc. Caregivers can also be anyone that has Power of Attorney over the client and assist the client with their health and financial decisions.

case management – where an agency provides a service to a client that connects them with services specified to their needs.

Children's Choice Waiver (CC) – a Medicaid program designated to those that are diagnosed as disabled and meets the program criteria to receive assistance under the program guidelines. This program is only available to children and the maximum age is 18 years old. There after the children will have to transition to the NOW Waiver Program.

Comprehensive Plan of Care (CPOC) – is documentation that is required in order to provide the client services. This document entails the client's demographic information, medical history, family, history, medications, psychiatric background, goals/limitations, support system, services needed, provider of services, budget, and signatures. This is a mandatory document that must be maintain annually as well as throughout the year with addendum updates.

Day Habilitation – a Medicaid entity that can be available to the client through a Medicaid Freedom of Choice Provider. Day Habilitation services are used to provide an opportunity for the client to interact with others. Day Habilitation services can be 8 hours a day 5 days a week or it can vary depending on the client.

direct service worker (DSW) – an employee of the Medicaid PCA provider agency that assist the client with daily living activities.

environmental modifications – a service provided by Medicaid contractors to assist the client with increasing mobility within the home. Services can range from bathroom modifications to ramps for better access into the home.

Freedom of Choice (FOC) – a list of Medicaid entities that a client can choose from in order to provide them a service.

independent living – when a client wants to live alone or detached from their caregiver. In some cases, it could be the client living in their own home, apartment, or manufactured home. Independently living could also mean the client wants to live on the property but have their own space.

Personal Care Attendant (PCA) Service – on the FOC list the direct service worker's provider will be listed under PCA. PCA agency what the

client and/or caregiver reference to when wants to have a dsw work within the home.

Personal Emergency Response System (PERS) – a service that provides emergency assistance to clients if needed. In the case a client lives alone and may spend several hours without assistance, they can use this service for an emergency. This service is connected to the client's phone line which allows the service provider to assist them in the case of an emergency.

provider – a Medicaid entity that is available on the FOC list to provide a service to Medicaid recipients.

respite care entity – a Medicaid service provider that can be used in the case the client's caregiver is going to be out of town or has an emergency that will require the client to need someone to

assist with monitoring the client over night or a duration of time.

revision – is used when services were not budgeted into the original CPOC budget and additional services are needed. This could include additional day habilitation hours, additional dsw hours, corrections to environmental modifications, etc. A revision can be made to any Medicaid FOC provider.

shared support – when two or more clients share a FOC provider service. This could include dsw hours in order to decrease the cost but provide a service to both clients simultaneously.

Supported Independent Living (SIL) – a service provided by PCA entities for clients that live independently but need assistance with maintaining their finances. This is a documented service that can be reflected by the client's bank account and their living situations. Although this is a service the provider agency can provide; the client still can make their own decisions concerning their finances. This is a way to assist them with maintain an adequate quality of life.

Support Waiver (SW) – a Medicaid service provided by PCA for those clients are considered high functioning. This service is used primarily to assist the client with finding employment and interact in day habilitation services.

transitioning – when a client that is a Medicaid recipient of the Children's Choice Waiver and have reached 18 years old. Clients are required to transfer to the New Opportunity Waiver services in order to continue the program.

References

Louisiana Department of Health & Hospitals | Kathy Kliebert, Secretary. (n.d.). Retrieved September 11, 2015, from http://www.dhh.state.la.us/index.cfm/subhome/11

Index

First the author would like to thank everyone for their support of her first publication. This is only the beginning for the author and she has a great deal of information to share in the near future. She wanted to give you, the reader an opportunity to express your thoughts about the book and the content. This section of the book is dedicated to your feedback. We would like to know if the content was helpful in any way. If you are an organization, please feel free to let us know if this book may have helped your organization thrive. We look forward to reading your emails and reviews. Thanks again for your support.

Feedback and reviews can be stated on the following websites and social media platforms.

Amazon

Facebook: Tranquil Artistry LLC

Instagram: Tranquil Artistry LLC

Google +: Tranquil Artistry

Email: tranquilartistry@gmail.com

This author wants to continue with great content for her readers. Please understand that she's very eclectic in her work. The books vary from Non-Fiction, Fiction, Children Books, etc. We look forward to your continued support and appreciate everyone that has worked together to bring the author's vision to light.

Upcoming Publications:

Case Management 101: Non-Clinical Tactics to Guiding Your Client to Adequate Care: HIV/AIDS Edition

This book is a continuation of Case Management 101. The author wanted to provide content that would reflect the additional experience that she has encountered as a case manager. In this edition she will talk about getting to know the population, working in rural areas, getting better acquainted with HIV/AIDS, dealing with death, clients that give up on life, confidentiality, etc. This book is a great guide for those that are interested in assisting clients that have been diagnosed with HIV or AIDS. If you want to read similar content as this book; the author continues with that strategy. She wants the book to quick and to the point; in order for you, the reader to start your job and assist your clients in receiving care.

White Rose Queen - Children Book

Two girls lose an influential person in their lives and they have a difficult time dealing with pain. They find themselves remembering the great times with that person and find their way to acceptance. Along the way they find themselves on a journey as well as finding their strength. This is a great book to help children deal with the loss of a loved one. It will take them on a magical journey and help them illuminate their imagination.

Her Heart's History – Fictional Trilogy Novel

This is the story of three curvaceous women that live diversified lifestyles. All three women go on a journey of learning more about themselves, what they want in a significant other, and their sexual desires. They find themselves relying on each other to get through the good, the bad, and the deadly. If you're interested in hot and steamy erotica, this is your book. Each curvaceous lady has their own short novel and as a finale which allows them to join together as a force to be reckoned with. Stay tuned for a thrilling ride with these curvaceous ladies.

www.ingramcontent.com/pod-product-compliance
Lightning Source LLC
Chambersburg PA
CBHW070257290326
41930CB00041B/2624